MOUNT TERROR

By Maeve Sisk

Gareth Stevens
PUBLISHING

Please visit our website, www.garethstevens.com. For a free color catalog of all our high-quality books, call toll free 1-800-542-2595 or fax 1-877-542-2596.

Library of Congress Cataloging-in-Publication Data

Sisk, Maeve.
Mount Terror / by Maeve Sisk.
 p. cm. — (Scariest places on Earth)
Includes index.
ISBN 978-1-4824-1157-7 (pbk.)
ISBN 978-1-4824-1158-4 (6-pack)
ISBN 978-1-4824-1156-0 (library binding)
1. Volcanoes — Juvenile literature. 2. Antarctica — Geography — Juvenile literature. 3. Ross Island (Ross Sea, Antarctica) — History. I. Sisk, Maeve T. II. Title.
QE521.3 S57 2015
551.2—d23

First Edition

Published in 2015 by
Gareth Stevens Publishing
111 East 14th Street, Suite 349
New York, NY 10003

Copyright © 2015 Gareth Stevens Publishing

Designer: Katelyn E. Reynolds
Editor: Therese Shea

Photo credits: Cover, p. 1 John Bortniak, NOAA/Wikipedia.com; cover, pp. 1–24 (background texture) Eky Studio/Shutterstock.com; cover, pp. 1–24 (creepy design elements) Dmitry Natashin/Shutterstock.com; p. 5 (image) Ben Cranke/The Image Bank/Getty Images; p. 5 (map) Alexrk2/Wikipedia.com; p. 7 NSF/Josh Landis, employee 1999-2001/Wikipedia.com; p. 9 Gordon Wiltsie/National Geographic/Getty Images; p. 11 (inset) Hulton Archive/Getty Images; p. 11 (main) Universal History Archive/Getty Images; p. 13 Graham Coton/The Bridgeman Art Library/Getty Images; p. 15 Popperfoto/Getty Images; p. 17 Shakki/Wikipedia.com; p. 19 Carsten Peter/National Geographic/Getty Images; p. 21 Gaelen Marsden/Wikipedia.com.

Printed in the United States of America

CPSIA compliance information: Batch #CS15GS: For further information contact Gareth Stevens, New York, New York at 1-800-542-2595.

CONTENTS

Words in the glossary appear in **bold** type the first time they are used in the text.

VOLCANO!

Mount Terror is located in Antarctica on the eastern part of Ross Island. It's a **volcano**! However, it hasn't been active in a really long time. "Terror" is a word that means a great amount of fear. Should we be afraid of Mount Terror?

The volcano wasn't actually named for its terrifying nature. However, there are many other reasons to fear both Mount Terror and the wild lands of Antarctica, as you'll learn in this book.

Mount Terror is considered to be an inactive volcano because it doesn't **erupt**. The hardened **lava** around it is about 1 million years old!

ROSS ISLAND

Ross Island is 43 miles (69 km) long and 45 miles (72 km) wide. Four volcanoes formed it: Mount Terror, Mount Erebus, Mount Terra Nova, and Mount Bird. When they erupted, the superhot lava that came out of Earth cooled and hardened. This is the rock that makes up the island.

Even though Mount Terror is no longer active, Mount Erebus, the largest volcano on Ross Island, still erupts. It spits out "lava bombs"! That doesn't make Ross Island any warmer, though. Antarctica is the coldest place on Earth.

FRIGHTENING OR FUN?

Even though Mount Erebus has a lava lake within it, the area around it doesn't get any warmer than −4°F (−20°C) in the summer!

You can see the **crater** of Mount Erebus in this photo. A lava lake is located in it. Mount Terror is in the background.

7

KILLER COLD

Would you be scared of a place where it's always dark? You might not want to visit Mount Terror during winter. It stays dark for several months straight! The temperatures on Ross Island can get as cold as –58°F (–50°C). It's not that much better in the summer. In fact, it rarely gets above freezing.

To add to that, Antarctic winds can gust more than 100 miles (160 km) per hour. This makes it feel even colder on top of Mount Terror!

Antarctic temperatures are very dangerous for people.
If they're not wearing the right clothes, they risk
freezing body parts or even losing their lives.

THE EXPEDITION

In 1839, British explorer James Clark Ross set out for Antarctica. He commanded two ships, the *Erebus* and *Terror*. The **expedition** wasn't easy. One of his men fell overboard and drowned. It was very hard breaking up the Antarctic ice to keep the ships moving. Ross called the ice "motionless and **menacing**."

In January 1841, Ross saw an island with a volcano puffing smoke, which he named Mount Erebus. Next to it was another volcano he called Mount Terror. That island later came to be called Ross Island after the explorer.

James Clark Ross named the two famous Antarctic volcanoes after his ships. He had explored the Arctic before his trip to the Antarctic.

ALMOST ICED IN

James Clark Ross's ships were badly smashed up by the ice and often needed repairs during the expedition. Though Ross wanted to keep exploring, he finally hit ice so solid and thick he knew they couldn't move any farther.

After 4 years and 5 months at sea, Ross and his men were lucky to return to England alive. Ross decided not to go on the next expedition of the *Erebus* and *Terror*, this time to the Arctic.

FRIGHTENING OR FUN?

The last trip of the *Erebus* and *Terror* was doomed. The ships became trapped in ice, and the crews' skeletons were found years later.

This painting shows James Clark Ross planting the British flag on Antarctica while dozens of penguins look on.

13

FIRST ATTEMPT

During his first expedition to Antarctica in 1902, Robert Falcon Scott of the British navy and his friend Dr. Edward Wilson climbed the **shoulder** of Mount Terror. Scott saw that the mainland seemed to go on and on. He began to think he could reach the South Pole, something no one had ever done before.

Scott, Wilson, and another British navy officer named Ernest Shackleton set out with a 19-dog sled team. Sickness and bad weather made them give up and turn back, however. Scott called the expedition a "nightmare."

The aim of Scott's first expedition was to map the land and gather scientific facts. He mentions Mount Terror several times in his writings. Pictured here from left to right are Ernest Shackleton, Robert Falcon Scott, and Edward Wilson.

SECOND TO THE SOUTH POLE

Robert Falcon Scott made a second expedition to the Antarctic to try again to reach the South Pole. He and his men reached Ross Island on January 4, 1911, and got to the South Pole on January 17, 1912.

However, another explorer, Roald Amundsen of Norway, had already planted his flag there. Disappointed, Scott and his crew headed back. Sadly, they died from hunger and cold before they could reach safety. Their bodies were found on November 12, 1912.

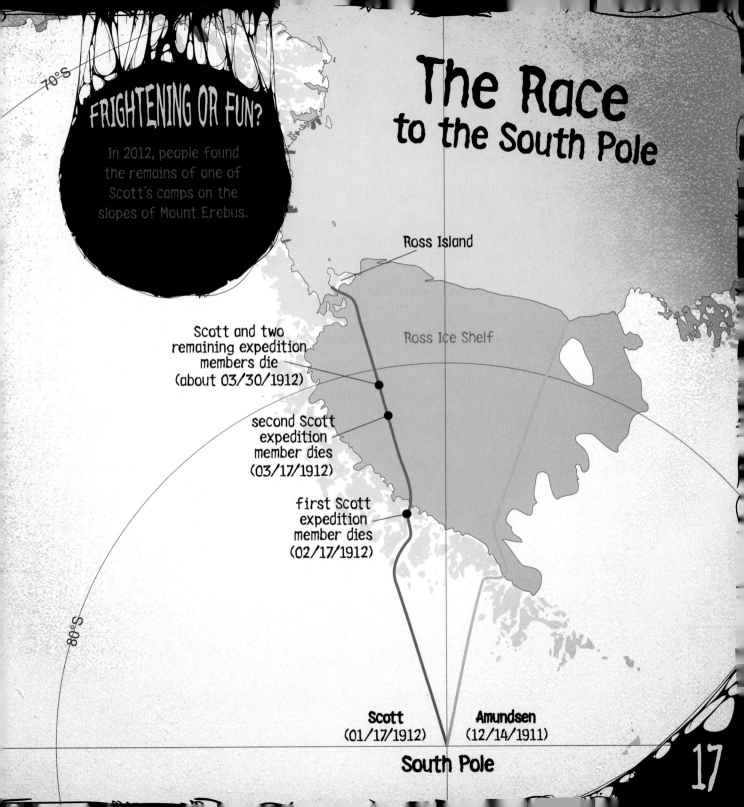

The Race
to the South Pole

FRIGHTENING OR FUN?

In 2012, people found the remains of one of Scott's camps on the slopes of Mount Erebus.

Ross Island

Ross Ice Shelf

Scott and two remaining expedition members die (about 03/30/1912)

second Scott expedition member dies (03/17/1912)

first Scott expedition member dies (02/17/1912)

80°S

Scott
(01/17/1912)

Amundsen
(12/14/1911)

South Pole

17

SKI
MOUNT TERROR?

Mount Terror has an **elevation** of 10,702 feet (3,262 m). It's also snowy all year round. That means that skiers see it as an ideal place to test their skills. They can expect to ski about 2 miles (3.2 km) downhill!

Unlike at most ski resorts, skiers in Antarctica have to make their way to the top without lifts and bundle up for the incredibly cold and windy conditions of Antarctica. Could you do it? Many people get terrified just thinking about it!

Both Mount Erebus and Mount Terror are on some skiers' must-do lists!

19

LIVING NEAR MOUNT TERROR

Scientists and visitors flying into Antarctica land on islands or on the coasts. Ross Island is one of the major **destinations**, and so many visitors can see Mount Terror for themselves.

The McMurdo Station is located near Mount Terror. As many as 1,000 people live there in the summer months. Only about 250 remain during the winter. It's often just too dangerous to go outside and work then. If you think you could deal with the terrible conditions of Antarctica, maybe a visit to McMurdo and Mount Terror is for you!

McMurdo Station is made up of about 85 buildings.
It's the largest community in all Antarctica.

GLOSSARY

crater: a bowl-shaped hole on the surface of a planet or moon

destination: the place to which somebody or something is going

elevation: height above sea level

erupt: burst forth

expedition: a trip made for a certain purpose

lava: hot, liquid rock that flows out of a volcano

menacing: seeming dangerous or capable of causing harm

shoulder: the slope near the top of a hill or mountain

volcano: an opening in a planet's surface through which hot, liquid rock sometimes flows

FOR MORE INFORMATION

Books

Bledsoe, Lucy Jane. *How to Survive in Antarctica*. New York, NY: Holiday House, 2006.

Friedman, Mel. *Antarctica*. New York, NY: Children's Press, 2009.

Llanas, Sheila Griffin. *Who Reached the South Pole First?* Mankato, MN: Capstone Press, 2011.

Websites

Cool Facts About Antarctica
faculty.umf.maine.edu/gretchen.legler/public.www/antarcticawebsite/coolf.htm
Learn much more about this harsh environment.

Robert Falcon Scott: Antarctic Explorer
enchantedlearning.com/explorers/page/s/scott.shtml
Read about the adventures of Robert Falcon Scott.

INDEX

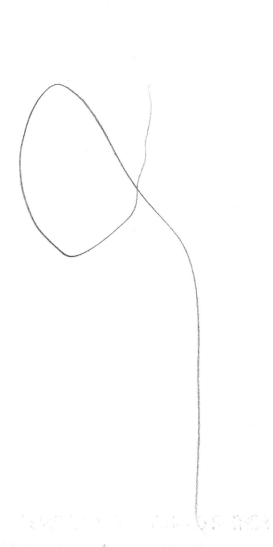